Le...
Desert Plants

Dot Barlowe

DOVER PUBLICATIONS, INC.
Mineola, New York

Bibliographical Note

Learning About Desert Plants is a new work, first published by Dover
Publications, Inc., in 2000.

International Standard Book Number: 0-486-41292-X

Manufactured in the United States of America
Dover Publications, Inc., 31 East 2nd Street, Mineola, N.Y. 11501

Introduction

One of the charms of the American desert is the blossoming of the dry, sandy landscape into a vast flower garden after a heavy rainfall. Delight in this beauty as you read about twelve desert plants found in our great American Southwest. All are important to the region's ecology, including its birds, mammals, and insects. As you read about each plant, you will be able to illustrate its page by placing a colorful sticker in the space provided. Perhaps you will be interested in finding out more about how the living things in the desert adapt to their difficult environment in order to survive.

Ocotillo

The ocotillo's red or white flowers bloom at the ends of long stems. Watch out—these stems have dangerously sharp thorns during the desert's dry season! Leaves grow at the base of the thorns after a rainfall. Some people plant the ocotillo as fencing because its thorns keep out intruders. The ocotillo grows in the rocky slopes and desert country of the American Southwest.

Saguaro

Waxy white flowers with golden centers bloom at the very top of the saguaro, the tallest cactus in the desert. It can reach a height of fifty feet! The saguaro stores enormous amounts of water. In addition, its fruit can be eaten. Birds like to nest in its branches, and moths, bats, and night-flying insects all thrive within its three-inch-wide flowers.

Desert Sage

Delicate purple flowers appear in clusters on this low-growing shrub. Its silvery leaves, when crushed, have a very pleasant fragrance. They are related to the cooking herb sage, but not to the sagebrush that also grows in the desert. The desert sage lives on the slopes of the rocky desert country as well as on the dry, level "flats." Mule deer like to graze near this plant.

Desert Five-Spot

The desert five-spot glows like a tiny pink lamp as the hot desert sun shines through it. Its fuzzy, heart-shaped leaves are topped by charming red-spotted flowers. The plant can grow to be about two feet tall. It grows on desert flats and washes (stream beds that remain dry until a rainfall). The desert five-spot blooms from March through May.

Desert Lily

Because of its white flowers, the desert lily is often mistaken for the Easter lily. This plant blooms on the desert's sandy flats and gentle slopes. Its waxy leaves grow close to the ground, but the stalk with its many flowers can reach six feet. Native Americans used the fleshy bulbs of the desert lily for food. It blooms from March to May.

Indian Blanket

The brilliant, showy, yellow-tipped red flowers of the Indian blanket would certainly catch your eye if you were driving along the desert roadside! The Indian blanket's colors remind people of the bright blankets woven by Native Americans. This plant may grow to be two and a half feet tall. It blooms from March to May. Outside the desert, it grows on dry, sandy plains.

Spanish Bayonet

The waxy flowers of the Spanish bayonet grow in magnificent masses at the top of the plant's heavy stalk. The sharply pointed leaves have long provided Native Americans with fibers to weave baskets, mats, cloth, and sandals. The buds and fruit are edible, and the roots can be used to make soap! It grows along the Rio Grande and in southwest Texas.

Fishhook Cactus

The spines of this small, round cactus protect it from creatures that would find it a tasty meal! Its long, curved spines look like fishhooks. The pretty crown of pink flowers blooms in April and May. It rarely grows taller than six inches. You might find a desert kangaroo rat making its home near this plant, which can be found in the desert and in dry grasslands.

Desert Sand Verbena

From February to July, especially after heavy winter rains, this delicate plant trails its violet-pink flowers along the sand. Its fuzzy leaves hug the ground and have adapted to prevent the plant's moisture from evaporating too quickly. Sand verbena is found in the dry grasslands of the desert. You might also find the desert tarantula nearby!

Spotted Langloisia

The tiny half-inch blossoms of this plant bring color to the stark desert landscape from April through June. It grows on hills among pine trees and near the creosote bushes of the desert. The plant stands about one-and-a-half to six inches tall. Its tough leaves sport sharp spines that protect it from a host of plant eaters. Lilac sunbonnet is another name for its tiny flowers.

Desert Mariposa Lily

From two to six of these beautiful tulip-shaped lilies grow in a cluster on the plant's short stem. The flowers can be yellow, orange, or bright red. Generally, mariposas (Spanish for "butterflies") that grow in California are dark red, while those in Arizona and Utah are shades of yellow or orange. This lily is found in rocky desert areas or in brushland.

Coulter's Lupine

When there is plenty of fall or winter rain in the southern Arizona desert, Coulter's lupine turns miles of landscape into a gorgeous blue and violet flower garden. This plant grows on rocky slopes and in open country as well as in the desert. It blooms from January to May along with other wildflowers, producing a magnificent bouquet.